The 5-Ingredient Vegetarian Cookbook

Easy, Simple and Delicious for Your Plant-Based Lifestyle

By Jennifer Walker

Table of Content

Introduction

I firmly believe every decision we make in life, regardless of how well-calculated the move is, has good and bad consequences. Your dietary habit is no exception; in fact, your food choices significantly impact overall health and wellbeing. Precisely, when it comes to dieting, the rule of thumb here is simple; proper nutrition results in healthy living and satisfaction.

However, we live in a world where new dietary habits crop up every day. Besides, today, people are redefining the old dietary practices to suit the modern lifestyle. New dietary habits, coupled with the complexity of today's lifestyle, put the world on a collision course with the principles of healthy living. What encourages me, however, is the fact that some dietary practices like vegetarianism have stood the test of time.

Vegetarianism has been around for quite a long time, but a lot of things about it have remained unchanged. Growing up as a vegetarian impelled my career decision to become a professional dietitian. My parents were staunch vegetarians who took not even a peep outside the boundaries of vegetarianism. One thing I learned from living with my parents is that ditching meat for vegetables is never natural.

However, if you have decided to go vegetarian life, congratulations, you have made a brilliant decision. This because commitment to vegetarianism is a dedication to good health. And luckily for you, I have written this book to hold your hand during the transition. The book will see you through the journey, opening up horizons of whole new meals that you will adore.

Regardless of your reason for going vegetarian, you will adore this cookbook. Whether it is for religious or health purposes, I have unpacked the information you need and served it up in a way that is easy to understand. Besides, I will give you cooking tips that will help you nail vegetarianism and make it part of your lifestyle. Trust me, the journey will be bumpy, but with this cookbook, you have a partner to keep you going even when things seem to be grinding to a halt.

As if that is not enough, this book has simple recipes to get you started. Everything from salads, appetizers, and mains, each method is designed to complement your health and those crazy cravings. I went for recipes with five ingredients or less, to give you a smooth ride in the kitchen. You can be sure to prepare stress-free weeknight dinners, lunches not forgetting brunches. People say, "More ingredients equal to more flavor" But that is a misconception. I have focused on the taste using fewer ingredients. Moreover, five elements are easy to buy and prepare.

Trust me, with this cookbook; you will love vegetables even before you know it. This cookbook is not only the best vegetarian book with tons of recipes but also a simple guide to vegetarianism and benefits to it. If looking forward to vegetarianism for the rest of your life, this cookbook is for you.

Chapter 1 Salad Over Streak: On Vegetarianism

What Is Vegetarianism?

Vegetarianism is voluntary abstinence from consumption of meat and sometimes by-products of animals. Vegetarians follow plant-based foods, including or excluding dairy and eggs in their foods. People practice vegetarianism for health issues, religion, or ethical reasons. Yogis, for example, believe that good and healthy food contains prana, a universal energy giver. Prana is abundant in grains, nuts, fruits, and vegetables. It is also believed that harming living things is spiritually unhealthy.

Some people also believe that taking animal life for any reason is unethical and sinful. Funny. Right? Healthy practitioners also believe that too much of proteins found in animal products may cause bone loss, kidney disease, or cancer. The list goes on and on, but at the end of the day, vegetarianism is tried and tested. It is not an entirely new diet habit, and when practiced right, the benefits are there for all to see.

Did You There Are Different Types Of Vegetarians?

Although vegetarianism is a plant-based eating pattern, there are multiple levels of it. The principal difference in types of vegetarianism manifest in what one picks from the allowable animal products. Below are examples of vegetarians based on the animal products they exclude from their diet.

Vegan

Vegans, unlike any other vegetarians, exclude all animal products from their food. The animal products are in the form of gelatin and honey. Vegans typically avoid animal products such as wool, leather, and silk.

Lacto-Ovo Vegetarian

"Lacto" and "ovo" are Latin words for milk and eggs, consecutively. A Lacto-Ovo vegetarian does not eat white or red meat, fish, or insects. They tend to consume free-range eggs and eggs from grass-fed birds

Lacto Vegetarian

Lacto vegetarians exclude white and red meat, fish, and eggs in their diet. However, they consume dairy products such as yogurt, cheese, and milk.

Ovo Vegetarian

On the other hand, ovo vegetarians do not eat white and red meat, fish, or dairy products. They consume eggs, products, and vegetables.

Flexitarian

The word flexitarian originates from the words flexible and vegetarian. Flexitarian is also referred to as semi-vegetarian. They primarily consume plant-based foods but occasionally enjoy meat in.

Proletarian

Proletarians are semi-vegetarians who choose to avoid red meat, fish, and other animal meats. However, proletarian consume chicken and any other poultry.

Pescatarian

If proletarians limit themselves to poultry, what do you call a vegetarian who limits themselves to fish? They are called pescatarian. Pescatarians avoid white and red meat but consume shellfish and fish.

Benefits Of Going Vegetarian

Many peoples' perception of life without meat is dull. However, this is a misguided perception, especially when you consider the number of benefits one can reap by going vegetarianism. Most importantly, vegetarianism is fun. If you are skeptical about vegetarianism, perhaps the following benefits will change your mind.

Weight Loss Benefit

If you are looking to lose weight, try vegetarian food. According to one study, a vegetarian diet lowers your body mass index (BMI) more effectively. Vegetarian food rings true — particularly if you have a habit of eating high-fat meats. Besides, other studies have shown that meatless foods have increased the life expectancy of overweight adults. However, the weight loss benefits do not come on a silver platter. You should endeavor to follow the general health guidelines like limiting added sugar, trans fats, and sugary drinks.

Lower Cancer Risk

Lowering the risk of cancer is another benefit of vegetarian food. Cancer is a chronic disease that is affecting many Americans. While there are many triggers for this disease, it is believed that eating habits could be driving you towards the menace.

Fortunately, if you are a vegetarian, you stand an excellent chance to live a cancer-free life.

One cancer management and research report revealed that people who eat meat-free foods lower the risk of cancer. Cancer risk is reduced because vegetable-rich meals provide plenty of antioxidants, fiber, and phytochemicals. Besides, vegetarians avoid processed meat, which is believed to accelerate several types of cancers.

Heart Health Benefits

Moreover, eating meatless meals lowers the risks of heart disease. In fact, according to the Harvard Health Publications, people who eat vegetarian foods have low-density lipoprotein (LDL) cholesterol and low blood pressure levels. Besides, the American Heart Association intimates that vegetarian foods can regulate blood pressure. Generally, plant-based foods tend to lower saturated fat, cholesterol, and total fat.

Diabetes Control

Another perk of eating vegetarian food is diabetes prevention and control. As you may have known, meat like other high-fat diets can make your body to develop insulin insensitivity. On the other hand, plant-based meals boost insulin sensitivity. Because of this, eating vegetarian foods can be an incredible way to put diabetes under control.

However, these benefits are not straight forward; there are several hurdles to overcome. For example, plant-based foods tend to be high in refined carbs, added sugar, calories, and saturated fat. All these factors combined can quickly negate the diabetes control effect of vegetarian diets.

Economic Benefits

The economic benefit may sound like cosmetic benefits, but it makes a lot of sense. Meat is very costly, especially if you like organic, antibiotic, and hormone-free brands. Eating a vegetarian diet helps you avoid the extra expense. One study found that plant-based foods can deliver cost savings of up to $750 annually. The best part is that even with these cost savings, you still get more nutrients.

Tips To a Successful Vegetarian Lifestyle

According to research, 84% of people return to consuming meat even after promising to go vegetarian. Imagine having been consuming meat all your life and then one day you decide to go vegetarian. Trust me; it can be hard. Below are some tips for success in a vegetarian journey.

Find Motivation

You must find a motivation to abstain from your favorite meat-based foods. For example, if you want to lose weight, think of your current body shape and the state of your health. Use the pain you are going through as the motivation to get you to the heights you want to reach. Vegetarian food can help you lose weight, a great motivation towards a vegetarian lifestyle.

Resist Temptation

Do not let food aromas entice you. Avoid internet pages that cover meat and dairy products. If you have food cravings, eat vegetarian food to your fullest. Most importantly, spend time looking for new vegetarian recipes.

Set a Date And Start Small

For a successful vegetarian lifestyle, set time on when to start. Set milestones that are achievable. A gradual approach to vegetarianism also works wonders. You may begin by eliminating poultry, red meat than fish in your food. You may even start with a few days of the week on when to go vegetarian then add the days gradually as you get used to the food.

Swap Ingredients

Going vegetarian does not mean you will abandon most of your favorite recipes. You can prepare your favorite food but with a touch of vegetarian food. Replace main proteins with vegetarian options. For example, you can replace dairy milk with almond or soy milk. Animal-based broth can also be replaced with vegetable broth. Great. Right?

Become Label Reader

Animal products can be sneaky. They hide in your grocery foods, so you need to be very careful. Familiarize yourself with hidden animal products. For example, honey is a bee product. Gelatin comes from animal collagen and, casein is derived from sheep or cow milk.

Chapter 2 The Vegetarian kitchen

The Five-Ingredient Pantry

Becoming a vegetarian does not mean that your foods will no longer be fun. It does not mean your meals will look like that of a bunny rabbit, either. There is a big world of vegetarian foods out there. It all starts with stocking your pantry with a wide range of foods. This way, you will make the veganism lifestyle easy and enjoyable. Here are some of the essential to add to your pantry:

Oil And Condiments

Oil is critical in every food you prepare. The type of oil you need depends on the dish you want to cook. I know some of these ingredients may be new to you, but you will soon become familiar with them. Some of the best oils and condiments for vegetarians include olive oil, grape seed oil, coconut oil, sesame oil, Asian herbs, barbecue sauce, and hot sauce.

Canned And Bottled Goods

With a vegetarian lifestyle, you will need to prepare and cook meals from scratch. However, sometimes, time will not be on your side; this is where canned foods come in handy.

Examples of canned and bottled foods include baked beans, spaghetti sauce, lemon, lime juice, enchilada sauce, tomato paste, sun-dried tomatoes, salsa and many more

Spices/ Seasonings

Spices and seasoning make your dishes come alive. Some recipes require dried spices and seasonings, while others come out perfectly with fresh herbs. Some of these flavorings are salt, pepper, chili, garlic, onion and ginger powder, lemons, limes, basil, cinnamon, cumin, parsley oregano, rosemary, cayenne, cardamom, cilantro, nutmeg, turmeric, and curry.

Nuts And Seeds

Nuts and seeds are great snacks and toppers. Having a vast assortment of them is of enormous advantage. For maximum freshness, consider storing nuts and seeds in a Mason jar in your refrigerator. Some of these nuts and seeds are almonds, chia seeds, pecans, pumpkin seeds, sesame seeds, walnuts, sunflower seeds, and hemp hearts.

Pasta/ Flours

Even if you are not baking, the powder will be essential in your kitchen. Thickening gravies and sauces will call for some powder. Pasta, on the other hand, is a typical food that can be cooked in a million ways. Some examples are noodles, pasta, almond flour, buckwheat flour, chickpea flour, and whole wheat flour.

Vegetarian Flavor Booster

Substituting meat with beans in your dishes and expecting the same outcome will significantly disappoint you. It is necessary to compensate taste in your vegetarian meals by the use of alternative flavor boosters. Flavor boosters bring out a satisfying vegetarian dish to cab all the non-vegetarian carvings.

Tomato Puree

If looking for a rich and meaty flavor in your meal, then potato puree is a must-have. Fry the tomato puree in fried onions to bring out the sweeter notes and eliminate the rawness.

Soy Sauce

Soy sauce comes from fermented soybean paste, brine and, grain. A splash of soy sauce to your meal is an excellent way to spice up the stews and casseroles. Soy sauces are of a wide variety, but the thicker and darker the soy sauce is, the richer the flavor.

Nutritional Yeast

Nutritional yeast is a staple in most vegetarians. It might not sound appetizing, but trust me, it is a fantastic flavor booster. It has a nutty, creamy, and cheesy flavor, which highly complements potatoes, salads, and stir-fries. Nutritional yeast can entirely substitute parmesan when sprinkled on meals.

Vegetable Stock

Vegetable stock is a distilled serum of various vegetables and tremendously adds flavor to food. The good news is you can make your vegetable stock instead of using stock cubes, which contain dubious ingredients. Using vegetable stock in place of water adds a huge flavor punch

Miso

Adding the paste to meals is an excellent idea of enhancing rich and deep flavor. Miso is a Japanese tradition seasoning made from salt and fermented soybeans. Dark miso has a stronger taste compared to the light miso. One of the best ways to use this miso is by preparing traditional miso soup. Be careful though the light miso has high sugar content.

Vegetarian Cooking Tips

Believe me, when I say cooking a hearty vegetarian meal is not rocket science. It is easy, and no professional trick is needed. Even when you need to prepare a typical meal for a considerable crowd; made of vegetarians and meat lovers, panic not. We have got you covered. The following vegetarian cooking tips will help you prepare meals that are both healthy and flavorful.

Build a Balanced Meal

Like non-vegetarians, vegetarians require a balanced meal. Combining veggies, protein, and starches in your meal helps you stay healthy and fuller for a long time. Fortunately, there are plenty of ways to cook balanced vegetarian meals. For example, you can prepare a turmeric rice bowl with chickpeas. You get protein from peas, starch from brown rice and, fiber from vegetables.

Include Umami Ingredients Or Get Spicy

It is not wise to get wrapped up in a salt-pepper routine since it will eventually get tiresome. So, go big in seasoning your vegetarian dishes and break free from the usual. Be generous when seasoning, no matter what the meal is. If you want rich flavors, you have to play big with the seasons. Right?

Build Up The Deep Flavor

Excite your vegetarian plate by mixing as many flavors as you can. As that beef roast takes deep characters during that aggressive roast, so are the veggies. The crispy, crunchy and crusty bits on browned vegetables add tons of flavor. Imagine a roasted whole head of cauliflower. It definitely would not be of a looker with the usual pale and milky florets.

Use Various Colors

Vegetables, unlike meat, come in an array of beautiful colors. From green kale to bright pink radishes, there is a whole color wheel to explore. Choose seasoning ingredients at their peak of ripeness. Ripeness ensures that their color pop in the meal.

Slow Roast Food

Slow cooking food removes water from them, intensifying the flavors and making their texture chewy. Imagine the difference in taste between sun-dried tomatoes and fresh tomatoes. Cooked meat is said to have sixty-five percent water, while veggies have eighty percent. A lot? Roasted squash is flavorful, bright, and satisfying compared to fried or boiled squash.

Chapter 3: 5 Ingredients Recipes

Appetizers Recipe

Chilled Bread and Almond Soup

Prep time: 10 minutes, Cook time: 2 minutes; Serves 4

5 Ingredients

2 ½ oz white bread

1 garlic clove

¼ Cup almonds, raw

1 tbsp white vinegar

2 Cups grapes

What you ' ll need from the store cupboard

3 tbsp olive oil

1 tbsp sea salt

Instructions

1. Soak the white bread in two cups of water in a bowl. Separate the bread crust from the middle part. Use the middle only for white results.

2. Add garlic, almond and a few tablespoons of water in your food processor then blend until smooth.

3. Add the soaked bread, white vinegar, olive oil, salt to taste and any remaining water. Blend until smooth.

4. Cool the soup in a fridge for two hours then serve with a handful of grapes.

5. Enjoy.

Nutrition Facts Per Serving

Calories 204, Total Fat 14g, Saturated Fat 2g, Total Carbs 18g, Net Carbs 15g, Protein 3g, Sugar 9g, Fiber 2g, Sodium 594mg, Potassium 156mg

Creamy Tomato Basil Soup

Prep time: 5 minutes, Cook time: 25 minutes; Serves 4

5 Ingredients

1 red onion, diced

2 garlic cloves, crushed

2 cans tomatoes, diced

1 cup basil, fresh

3 ⅕ oz Greek yogurt

What you' ll need from the store cupboard

3 tbsp olive oil

3 cups vegetable broth

1 tbsp tomato paste

2 tbsp honey

Salt to taste

Hard cheese of choice

Spicy sauce of choice

Instructions

1. Cook the onions with olive oil in a large saucepan over medium heat for five minutes.

2. Add garlic and cook for thirty seconds.

3. Add tomatoes and vegetable broth then simmer for twenty minutes.

4. Cut the fresh basil and add it to the soup.

5. Add yogurt, tomato paste, and honey to the soup then hand blend until smooth.

6. Add salt to taste.

7. You may also add grated cheese and spicy sauce if you desire.

8. Serve and enjoy

Nutrition Facts Per Serving

Calories 80, Total Fat 2g, Saturated Fat 2g, Total Carbs 14g, Net Carbs 11g, Protein 5g, Sugar 8g, Fiber 3g, Sodium 1147mg, Potassium 234mg

Supreme Pear Soup

Prep time: 3 minutes, Cook time: 12 minutes; Serves 4

5 Ingredients

1 ½ tbsp flour

2 garlic cloves

½ tbsp cinnamon, ground

4 pear, roughly sliced

¼ cup walnuts

What you ' ll need from the store cupboard

1 ½ tbsp butter

1 ½ tbsp sugar

2 cups water

3 ½ blue cheese

Instructions

1. Melt the butter and mix with flour until a smooth mixture is obtained.

2. Add the cloves, cinnamon, sugar, water and pear pieces then heat until bubbling. Simmer for five minutes.

3. Use a hand blender to blend until smooth.

4. Crumble the walnuts, and blue cheese then use them to garnish the soup.

5. Serve and enjoy.

Nutrition Facts Per Serving

Calories 303, Total Fat 16g, Saturated Fat 7g, Total Carbs 35g, Net Carbs 27g, Protein 7g, Sugar 22g, Fiber 6g, Sodium 391mg, Potassium 302mg

White Bean Spread

Prep time: 8 minutes, Cook time: 2 minutes; Serves 2

5 Ingredients

1 medium onion, roughly chopped

1 garlic clove, roughly chopped

1 can white beans

2 tbsp parsley, fresh and chopped

2 tbsp chives, fresh and chopped

What you'll need from the store cupboard

2 tbsp olive oil

½ juiced lemon

¼ Cup tomatoes, sun-dried in oil

1 tbsp water

Salt and pepper to taste

2 tbsp tomato puree

Worcestershire sauce

Instructions

1. Fry the onion and cloves in olive oil until lightly browned.

2. Transfer to a mixing bowl.

3. Drain and rinse the canned beans then add them to the bowl.

4. Add the lemon juice and all other ingredients to the mixing bowl. Use a hand blender to blend until smooth.

5. Serve with whole-meal bread. Enjoy.

Nutrition Facts Per Serving

Calories 327, Total Fat 16g, Saturated Fat 2g, Total Carbs 42g, Net Carbs 29g, Protein 13g, Sugar 3g, Fiber 12g, Sodium 476mg, Potassium 795mg

Cashew Cream

Prep time: 5 minutes, Cook time: 0 minutes; Serves 5

5 Ingredients

1 ¼ cup cashews

1 tbsp soy sauce

1 tbsp mustard

¼ tbsp aniseed, ground

1 tbsp caraway seeds

What you ' ll need from the store cupboard

¼ tbsp pepper

½ cup of water

3 tbsp lemon juice

Instructions

1. Add cashews, soy sauce, mustard, aniseed and pepper in a blender. Blend until smooth.

2. Add water until the desired consistency is achieved.

3. Pour in a glass jar then refrigerate for four to five days.

4. Add a quarter cup of water and one tablespoon of lemon juice then blend. Add a tablespoon of caraway seeds.

5. Now cashew cream can be used as a coleslaw dressing.

Nutrition Facts Per Serving

Calories 183, Total Fat 14g, Saturated Fat 2g, Total Carbs 50g, Net Carbs 10g, Protein 6g, Sugar 2g, Fiber 1g, Sodium 83mg, Potassium 222mg

Cucumber Sandwiches With Cream Cheese

Prep time:5 minutes, Cook time:0 minutes; Serves 2

5 Ingredients

2 tbsp butter

2 tbsp cream cheese

4 slices soft bread

¼ cucumber

2 tbsp dill, fresh

What you＇ll need from the store cupboard

¼ tbsp salt

¼ tbsp pepper

Instructions

1. Spread butter on two bread slices and cream cheese on the other two slices.

2. Peel the cucumber then thinly slice it. Layer the slices on the buttered bread.

3. Dash salt and pepper as you desire on the cucumber slices.

4. Sprinkle over fresh dill then slap the cream cheese bread on the cucumber bread.

5. Serve and enjoy.

Nutrition Facts Per Serving

Calories 307, Total Fat 18g, Saturated Fat 10g, Total Carbs 29g, Net Carbs 23g, Protein 7g, Sugar 4g, Fiber 2g, Sodium 730mg, Potassium 172mg

Tortellini Soup

Prep time: 5 minutes, Cook time: 20 minutes; Serves 4

5 Ingredients

4 cups marinara sauce

1tbsp garlic, minced

⅛ tbsp red pepper flakes

2 cups tortellini cheese

Parmesan cheese for serving

What you ' ll need from the store cupboard

2 cups vegetable stock

1 cup spinach, chopped and frozen

½ tbsp oregano, dried

Instructions

1. Add vegetable stock, spinach, marinara sauce, and seasoning to your pot. Bring to boil.

2. Reduce heat and add tortellini cheese.

3. Cook until the cheese has cooked through.

4. Serve with parmesan cheese and enjoy.

Nutrition Facts Per Serving

Calories 237, Total Fat 5g, Saturated Fat 1g, Total Carbs 39g, Net Carbs 32g, Protein 11g, Sugar 12g, Fiber 5g, Sodium 1990mg, Potassium 893mg

Vegetarian Bok Choy Soup

Prep time:1 minute, Cook time:3 minutes; Serves 1

5 Ingredients

2 bok choy stalks

1 cup vegetable broth

1 tbsp nutritional yeast

2 dashes garlic powder

2 dashes onion powder

What you 'll need from the store cupboard

Salt to taste

Pepper to taste

Instructions

1.   Roughly chop the bok Choy stalks and add it into a microwave-safe bowl.

2.   Add all other ingredients and mix well.

3.   Place the bowl in your microwave for three minutes.

4.   Serve and enjoy.

Nutrition Facts Per Serving

Calories 28, Total Fat 0g, Saturated Fat 0g, Total Carbs 4g, Net Carbs 2g, Protein 2g, Sugar 2g, Fiber 1g, Sodium 205mg, Potassium 0mg

Coconut Noodle Soup

Prep time: 5 minutes, Cook time: 10 minutes; Serves 3

5 Ingredients

1 sweet potato, sliced

1 tbsp ginger, chopped

1 pack noodles

1 cup of coconut milk

1 tbsp cilantro for garnish, chopped

What you' ll need from the store cupboard

3 cups vegetable broth

¼ tbsp salt

Instructions

1. Add vegetable broth into a pot and heat under medium heat.

2. Add the sweet potato and ginger and bring to boil. Simmer until the sweet potato is tender.

3. Add noodles, milk, and salt to taste then cook until the noodles are heated through.

4. Adjust seasoning if you desire then garnish your soup with cilantro.

5. Serve and enjoy.

Nutrition Facts Per Serving

Calories 224, Total Fat 16g, Saturated Fat 13g, Total Carbs 16g, Net Carbs 11g, Protein 7g, Sugar 6g, Fiber 4g, Sodium 607mg, Potassium 556mg

Vegetarian Chilli with Mushroom and Beans

Prep time: 10 minutes, Cook time: 25 minutes; Serves 2

5 Ingredients

½ onion, diced

2 garlics

5 oz mushroom

15 oz black bean

2 tbsp red chili powder

What you ' ll need from the store cupboard

1 tbsp food oil

1 ½ cups water

2 tomato puree

Instructions

1. Heat oil in a saucepan then adds onion and garlic. Cook until soft.

2. Add mushrooms and cook until soft.

3. Add beans, chili powder and water then reduce the heat. Simmer while stirring occasionally.

4. Add the tomato puree and cook for ten more minutes. Reduce heat to low and leave it covered.

5. Serve when hot and enjoy.

Nutrition Facts Per Serving

Calories 312, Total Fat 1g, Saturated Fat 0g, Total Carbs 56g, Net Carbs 31g, Protein 20g, Sugar 1g, Fiber 20g, Sodium 10mg, Potassium 838mg

Spiced Carrot And Red Lentil Soup

Prep time: 10minutes, Cook time: 2 minutes; Serves 4

5 Ingredients

2 carrots, chopped

1 onion, chopped

1 garlic, grated

1 cup red lentils, dried

5 cups vegetable broth

1 cup yogurt, natural

What you ' ll need from the store cupboard

1 tbsp olive oil

5 cups vegetable broth

Salt and pepper to taste

1 lemon juice

Instructions

1. Heat oil in a pot over low heat.

2. Add the onion, carrot, and garlic to the pot and cook for a minute.

3. Add the lentils and stir until they open the pores.

4. Add stock and yogurt then reduce heat to low. Simmer for fifteen minutes

5. Season with salt and pepper and add lemon juice.

6. Use a hand blender to blend the soup.

7. Serve with favorite herbs.

Nutrition Facts Per Serving

Calories 534, Total Fat 12g, Saturated Fat 3g, Total Carbs 79g, Net Carbs 45g, Protein 28g, Sugar 17g, Fiber 30g, Sodium 2456mg, Potassium 1324mg

Carrot And Ginger Soup

Prep time: 5 minutes, Cook time: 4 minutes; Serves 2

5 Ingredients

6 carrots, chopped

1small ginger, fresh

1 tbsp turmeric

1 tbsp cumin

½ tbsp cayenne pepper

What you' ll need from the store cupboard

2 tbsp sour cream

1 ½ cup vegetable broth

2 oranges, juiced

Salt and pepper to taste

Instructions

1. Add all the ingredients in a blender and blend until smooth.

2. Heat your saucepan and add the puree to cook for five minutes.

3. Let simmer then serve with bread and garnish with parsley. Enjoy

Nutrition Facts Per Serving

Calories 169, Total Fat 1g, Saturated Fat 0g, Total Carbs 37g, Net Carbs 28g, Protein 4g, Sugar 23g, Fiber 8g, Sodium 839mg, Potassium 889mg

Salads Recipe

White Bean Salad

Prep time: 3 minutes, Cook time: 0 minutes; Serves 2

5 Ingredients

1 can white beans, small

2 handful lambs lettuce

1 tbsp mustard

1 tbsp agave syrup

1 tbsp balsamic vinegar

What you ' ll need from the store cupboard

1 orange

2 tbsp olive oil

½ tbsp thyme

1 pinch salt

Instructions

1. Drain the white beans then rinse them.

2. Wash the lettuce thoroughly.

3. Peel and slice the orange.

4. Mix all the ingredients in a bowl.

5. All done, your salad is now ready. Serve and enjoy.

Nutrition Facts Per Serving

Calories 360, Total Fat 15g, Saturated Fat 2g, Total Carbs 45g, Net Carbs 35g, Protein 14g, Sugar 10g, Fiber 9g, Sodium 60mg, Potassium 1077mg

Quick White Bean Salad

Prep time: 10 minutes, Cook time: 0 minutes; Serves 4

5 Ingredients

1 can white beans

1 red onion

1 bell pepper, red

1 handful parsley, fresh

1 handful cilantro, fresh

What you ' ll need from the store cupboard

4 tomatoes, sun-dried

3 tbsp olive oil

1 tbsp lemon juice

Salt to taste

Pepper to taste

Instructions

1. Drain the beans and rinse them.
2. Dice the onions.
3. Wash the pepper and slice it into small pieces.
4. Slice the sun-dried tomatoes into small strips.
5. Add all the five ingredients with tomatoes into a bowl.
6. Add olive oil, lemon juice, then season with salt and pepper.
7. Serve with whole wheat bread if you desire.

Nutrition Facts Per Serving

Calories 389, Total Fat 22g, Saturated Fat 3g, Total Carbs 40g, Net Carbs 23g, Protein 12g, Sugar 13g, Fiber 15g, Sodium 227mg, Potassium 1107mg

Easy Green Bean Salad

Prep time: 10 minutes, Cook time: 0 minutes; Serves 4

5 Ingredients

1 jar green beans, medium

2 tbsp vinegar

1 tbsp sugar

1 handful parsley

1 red onion

What you' ll need from the store cupboard

3 tbsp olive oil

½ tbsp salt

½ tbsp pepper

Instructions

1. Drain the green beans and save the drained water.
2. Thinly slice the onion then put it in a large bowl. Add the drained beans in the bowl.
3. Chop parsley and add it along with other ingredients in the bowl.
4. Mix the ingredients then let rest for two to three hours.
5. Serve and enjoy.

Nutrition Facts Per Serving

Calories 254, Total Fat 21g, Saturated Fat 2g, Total Carbs 15g, Net Carbs 11g, Protein 2g, Sugar 8g, Fiber 4g, Sodium 592mg, Potassium 312mg

Supercharging Avocado Chickpea Salad

Prep time: 5 minutes, Cook time: 0 minutes; Serves 2

5 Ingredients

1 can chickpeas

2 avocados

1 handful cilantro

½ red onion

½ cup feta cheese

What you' ll need from the store cupboard

1lime juice

Salt to taste

Pepper to taste

Instructions

1. Drain the chickpeas and rinse them.

2. Dice the avocados and chop the cilantro.

3. Dice the onion then throw the chickpeas, cilantro, and onion in a large bowl.

4. Add cheese and lime juice to the bowl.

5. Season with salt and pepper to taste then mix the ingredients.

6. Serve and enjoy.

Nutrition Facts Per Serving

Calories 708, Total Fat 46g, Saturated Fat 12g, Total Carbs 57g, Net Carbs 32g, Protein 19g, Sugar 4g, Fiber 22g, Sodium 420mg, Potassium 1432mg

Watermelon Salad

Prep time: 5 minutes, Cook time: 0 minutes; Serves 3

5 Ingredients

3 cups cubed melon

3 tbsp rice vinegar

1 tbsp fresh basil, sliced thinly

1 tbsp fresh mint, chopped

1 tbsp fresh cilantro, chopped

What you'll need from the store cupboard

Sea salt to taste

Instructions

1. Place the watermelon in a colander then sprinkle salt as you toss the watermelon.

2. Let it rest so that some liquid will drain out.

3. Toss the watermelon with rice vinegar; 1 tablespoon of vinegar per one cup of melon.

4. Add the herbs and mix well to combine.

5. Serve and enjoy it when cold.

Nutrition Facts Per Serving

Calories 48, Total Fat 0g, Saturated Fat 0g, Total Carbs 12g, Net Carbs 9g, Protein 1g, Sugar 10g, Fiber 1g, Sodium 3mg, Potassium 181mg

Heavenly Halloumi Salad

Prep time: 5 minutes, Cook time: 20 minutes; Serves 3

5 Ingredients

⅔ Cup quinoa

2 cups arugula

1 can chickpeas

1 tbsp sweet paprika

5 oz halloumi cheese, chopped

What you ' ll need from the store cupboard

4 tbsp olive oil

1 lime juice

1 tbsp salt

Instructions

1. Follow the package *Instructions* to cook the quinoa.

2. Drain the chickpeas and rinse them.

3. Wash the arugula and put them in a large bowl.

4. Mix lime juice and zest with half of the olive oil. Add paprika and mix well.

5. Fry the cheese in the remaining oil for two minutes on each side.

6. Combine the cooked quinoa with chickpeas and arugula.stir in the lime mix.

7. Serve in small bowls with cheese on top. Enjoy.

Nutrition Facts Per Serving

Calories 598, Total Fat 36g, Saturated Fat 11g, Total Carbs 48g, Net Carbs 36g, Protein 24g, Sugar 1g, Fiber 10g, Sodium 1769mg, Potassium 517mg

5-Ingredient Vegetable Fried Brown Rice

Prep time: 5 minutes Cook time: 15 minutes; serves 4

Ingredients

1 cup mixed vegetables (frozen)

2 cups brown rice (cooked)

2 lightly whisked eggs

¼ - ⅓ cup of soy sauce (low-sodium)

What you'll need from store cupboard

1 tbsp coconut oil

Salt to taste

Fresh ground pepper to taste

Instructions

1. Heat oil in a frying pan (large) over medium-high heat.

2. Add mixed vegetables then cook for about 2 minutes while stirring.

3. Add rice and soy sauce. Cook for about 5 minutes until heated through.

4. Make a well in the mixture center then add eggs to the frying pan.

5. Let the eggs cook and set for about 1 minute then use a spoon to break them up into small pieces.

6. Season with additional soy sauce, pepper, and salt to taste.

7. Serve with sriracha and enjoy.

Nutritional Facts Per Serving

Calories: 279, total fat: 8g, saturated fat: 1.6g, total carbs: 45.8g, net carbs: 40.8g, Protein: 10.5g, sugars: 5.3g, dietary fiber: 5g, sodium: 524mg, potassium: 211.3mg

Garlic Roasted Carrots

Prep time: 5 minutes Cook time: 40 minutes serves: 6

Ingredients

24 baby carrots (tops 2-inches trimmed)

2 tbsp balsamic vinegar

5 cloves minced garlic

1 tbsp thyme (dried)

2 tbsp parsley leaves (chopped)

What you'll need from store cupboard

2 tbsp olive oil

Kosher salt to taste

Black pepper (freshly ground) to taste

Instructions

1. Preheat your oven to 350^0 F.

2. Coat a baking sheet with nonstick spray.

3. Place carrots on the baking sheet in a single layer.

4. Add vinegar, olive oil, garlic, and thyme then season with pepper and salt.

5. Toss gently to combine then place in the oven.

6. Bake for about 40 minutes until tender.

7. Garnish with parsley and serve immediately.

8. Enjoy!

Nutritional Facts Per Serving

Calories: 59.5, total fat: 4.6g, saturated fat: 0.6g, total carbs: 4.3g, net carbs: 3.3g, protein: 0.4g, sugars: 2.3g, dietary fiber: 1g, sodium: 25.8mg, potassium: 119mg

Baked Parmesan Mushrooms

Prep time: 10 minutes Cook time: 15 minutes; serves 4

Ingredients

1½ lb cremini mushrooms, thinly sliced

¼ cup lemon juice (freshly squeezed) + zest (from 1 lemon)

3 minced garlic cloves

¼ cup parmesan (grated)

2 tbsp thyme (dried)

What you'll need from store cupboard

3 tbsp olive oil

Kosher salt to taste

Black pepper (freshly ground) to taste

Instructions

1. Preheat your oven to 350^0 F.

2. Coat a baking sheet with nonstick spray.

3. Place mushrooms on the baking sheet in a single layer.

4. Add olive oil, lemon zest, lemon juice, garlic, parmesan, and thyme then season with pepper and salt.

5. Toss gently to combine and place in the oven.

6. Bake for about 15 minutes until tender and browned. Toss occasionally.

7. Serve immediately and enjoy.

Nutritional Facts per Serving

Calories: 163.5, total fat: 12.2g, saturated fat: 2.5g, total carbs: 10.3g, net carbs: 8.8g, protein: 6.9g, sugars: 3.4g, dietary fiber: 1.5g, sodium: 117.4mg, potassium: 794mg

Buttery Garlic GreenBeans

Prep time: 10 minutes Cook time: 10 minutes; serves 4

Ingredients

1 lb trimmed and halved fresh green beans

3 minced garlic cloves

2 pinches lemon pepper

What you'll need from store cupboard

3 tbsp butter

Salt to taste

Instructions

1. Place fresh green beans in a skillet (large) then cover with water. Boil over medium-high heat.

2. Reduce to medium-low heat and simmer the beans for about 5 minutes until beans to soften lightly.

3. Drain excess water then add butter and cook for about 3 minutes while stirring until butter melts.

4. Add garlic, stir and cook for about 4 minutes until garlic is fragrant and tender.

5. Season with salt and lemon pepper.

Nutritional Facts per Serving

Calories: 116, total fat: 8.8g, saturated fat: 6g, total carbs: 8.9g, net carbs: 5g, protein: 2.3g, sugars: 2g, dietary fiber: 3.9g, sodium: 222mg, potassium: 250mg

Roasted Butternut Squash Puree

Prep time: 15 minutes Cook time: 45 minutes serves: 4

Ingredients

1 large seeded and halved butternut squash

2 cups chicken stock

What you'll need from store cupboard

Salt to taste

Black pepper (ground) to taste

Instructions

1. Preheat your oven to 400^0 F.

2. Place the squash on a baking sheet with the flesh side up.

3. Roast in the oven for about 45-60 minutes until slightly brown and tender. Cool until it can be easily handled.

4. Scoop the squash flesh into a blender and blend until smooth.

5. Add ¼ cup chicken stock at a time while blending until smooth.

6. Season with pepper and salt.

7. Serve and enjoy.

Nutritional Facts per Serving

Calories: 159, total fat: 0.6g, saturated fat: 0.2g, total carbs: 40.3g, net carbs: 33.5g, protein: 3.7g, sugars: 8g, fiber: 6.8g, sodium: 395mg, potassium: 1203mg

Jamie's Sweet and Easy Corn on the Cob

Prep time: Cook time: 10 minutes serves: 6

Ingredients

2 tbsp white sugar

1 tbsp lemon juice

6 ears corn on the cob (silk and husks removed)

What you'll need from store cupboard

Instructions

1. Pour water into a large pot to about ¾ full and boil.

2. Add sugar and lemon juice and stir until sugar dissolves.

3. Place the ears of corn gently to the boiling water.

4. Turn off heat, cover the pot, and let the ears of corn cook for about 10 minutes until tender in hot water.

5. Serve and enjoy.

Nutritional Facts per Serving

Calories: 94, total fat: 1.1g, saturated fat: 0g, total carbs: 21.5g, net carbs: 19.1g, protein: 2.9g, sugars: 7g, dietary fiber: 2.4g, sodium: 14mg, potassium: 256mg

Entrees Recipe

5-Ingredients Coconut Curry

Prep time: 5 minutes Cook time: 10 minutes serves: 4

Ingredients

2 broccoli heads (small)

1 can coconut milk

2 tbsp red curry paste

1 can rinsed and drained chickpeas

12 tbsp cornstarch dissolved in 2 tbsp water (cold)

What you'll need from store cupboard

1 tbsp oil

Instructions

1. Sauté broccoli using 1 tbsp oil for a few minutes then add coconut milk.

2. Simmer for about 5-8 minutes. Make sure broccoli softens but tender-crisp.

3. Add curry paste and whisk to combine with coconut milk.

4. Add chickpeas and bring to boil (slight) then add cornstarch. Boil for a minute.

5. Reduce heat and let the mixture to slightly cool. The sauce will thicken.

6. Serve and enjoy.

Nutritional Facts per Serving

Calories: 506, total Fat: 21.5g, saturated fat: 17.2g, total carbs: 62.6g, net carbs: 44.3g, protein: 21.1g, sugars: 9.9g, dietary fiber: 14.3g, sodium: 241.2mg, potassium: 789mg

Smoked Mackerel & Leek Hash with Horseradish

Prep time: 10 minutes Cook time: 20 minutes serves: 2

Ingredients

8 oz halved potatoes

2 large and thinly sliced leeks

3 0z smoked mackerel (peppered and skin removed)

4 eggs

2 tbsp horseradish (creamed)

What you'll need from store cupboard

2 tbsp oil

A pinch of salt

Instructions

1. Place a splash of water in a bowl (microwaveable) then add potatoes.

2. Cover and cook for about 5 minutes on high until potatoes become tender.

3. In the meantime, heat the oil in a pan (frying) over medium heat.

4. Add leeks, a pinch of salt then cook for about 10 minutes until softened while stirring to prevent them from sticking.

5. Transfer the potatoes to the pan and fry for few minutes over high heat until a bit crisp.

6. Flake the mackerel through then divide the leek mixture to four indents.

7. Crack an egg into each indent, season and cover the pan.

8. Cook for about 8 minutes until egg whites are set and yolks runny.

9. Serve horseradish on the side and pan in the middle of the table.

Nutritional Facts per Serving

Calories: 546, total fat: 31.8g, saturated fat: 6.7g, total carbs: 34.6g, net carbs: 29.5g, proteins: 26.6g, sugars: 6.8g, dietary fiber: 5.1g, sodium: 237mg, potassium: 1024mg

Refried Bean Poblanos with Cheese

Prep time: 7 minutes Cook time: 6 minutes serves: 4

Ingredients

4 poblano chiles (seeded and halved)

1 can (16-ounce) refried beans (fat-free)

12 cups Picante sauce

1 cup Mexican blend cheese (pre-shredded reduced-fat4-cheese)

What you'll need from store cupboard

9 oz long-grain rice (microwaveable cooked)

Instructions

1. Place the chiles on a round plate (microwave-safe) cut sides up then cover the plate with a wax paper. Microwave for about 3 minutes on high.

2. Meanwhile, combine rice, beans, and Picante sauce in a bowl (medium). Stir well.

3. Evenly spoon the bean mixture into each chile halve then cover each with wax paper — microwave for about 2 minutes on high.

4. Uncover the chiles and sprinkle each with 2 tbsp cheese. Microwave for about 2 minutes on high until the cheese melts.

5. Serve and enjoy!

Nutritional Facts per Serving

Calories: 386, total fat: 10.1g, saturated fat: 6.1g, total carbs: 60g, net carbs: 55.2g, protein: 14g, sugars: 2.8g, dietary fiber: 4.8g, sodium: 336mg, potassium: 342mg

Grilled Heirloom Tomato and Goat Cheese Pizza

Prep time: 11 minutes Cook time: 4 minutes serves: 6

Ingredients

1 can (13.8-ounce) pizza crust dough (refrigerated)

1 halved garlic clove

1 large seeded and chopped heirloom tomato

2 oz part-skim mozzarella cheese (shredded)

3 oz herbed goat cheese (crumbled)

What you'll need from store cupboard

Cooking spray

Instructions

1. Prepare a grill to medium-high heat.

2. In the meantime, spread out the dough onto a baking sheet (large and coated with cooking spray).

3. Pat the dough into rectangles of 12 x 9-inch then lightly coat each with cooking spray.

4. Coat a grill rack with cooking spray.

5. Place the dough on a grill rack and grill for about 1 minute until browned lightly.

6. Turn the crust over, rub with the garlic clove and splash with tomato and cheeses.

7. Close the grill lid and grill for about 3 minutes.

8. Serve immediately.

Nutritional Facts per Serving

Calories: 243, total fat: 16.6g, saturated fat: 7g, total carbs: 14.8g, net carbs: 13.6g, proteins: 8.9g, sugars: 0.6g, dietary fiber: 1.2g, sodium: 261mg, potassium: 52mg

Grilled Cheese with Pepper and Onions

Prep time: 5 minutes Cook time: 8 minutes serves: 1

Ingredients

Cheese to taste

2 slices sourdough bread

½ Roasted poblano pepper (thinly sliced)

What you'll need from store cupboard

2 tbsp caramelized onions

2 tbsp butter (for cooking)

Instructions

1. Arrange the cheese evenly over the bread slices.

2. Top with caramelized onions and poblano slices. Cover with other bread side.

3. Place 1 tbsp butter in a skillet over medium heat. Swirl the butter around the pan until it melts.

4. Place the bread sandwich in the skillet then cook for a couple of minutes until golden brown on the bottom side. Put aside.

5. Add the remaining butter to the skillet and swirl to melting

6. Place the sandwich back with the cooked side up and cook the other side until golden brown.

7. Slice to half and enjoy!

Nutritional Facts per Serving

Calories: 509, total fat: 28.5g, saturated fat: 18.2, total carbs: 49.6g, net carbs: 47.1g, protein: 20.7g, sugars: 2.6g, dietary fiber: 2.5g, sodium: 797mg, potassium: 119mg

Desserts Recipe

Pineapple Orange Sorbet

Prep time: 20 minutes Cook time: 10 minutes serves: 10

Ingredients

½ cup sugar (granulated)

20 oz pineapple (crushed)

2 tbsp orange zest (freshly grated)

2 cups orange juice

1 tbsp lemon juice

What you'll need from store cupboard

½ cup of water

Instructions

1. Simmer water and sugar in a saucepan (medium) over medium-high heat. Make sure sugar dissolves.

2. Meanwhile, blend pineapple with its juice in a blender until smooth then transfer to a bowl (metal).

3. Add syrup, orange zest, orange juice, and lemon juice. Stir well.

4. Freeze the mixture until slightly firm. Make sure the mixture is not frozen.

5. Transfer the mixture to a blender and blend until smooth.

6. Transfer the mixture into a freezer container and freeze for about 2 hours until firm.

7. Serve and enjoy.

Nutritional Facts Per Serving

Calories: 95, total fat: 0.1g, saturated fat: 0g, total carbs: 24.2mg, net carbs:23.6g, protein: 0.6g, sugars: 22g, dietary fiber: 0.6g, sodium: 1mg, potassium: 170mg

Strawberries with Balsamic Vinegar

Prep time: 10 minutes Cook time: 1 hour serves: 6

Ingredients

16 oz large and hulled strawberries (fresh and cut in half)

¼ cup white sugar

2 tbsp balsamic vinegar

What you'll need from store cupboard

¼ tbsp black pepper (freshly ground) to taste

Instructions

1. Place the strawberries in a medium bowl then splash with sugar and drizzle with vinegar. Gently stir to combine.

2. Cover then let sit for about 1 hour at room temperature. Do not exceed 4 hours.

3. Grind black pepper over the berries and serve.

Nutritional facts per serving

Calories: 60, total fat: 0.2g, saturated fat: 0g, total carbs: 14.9g, net carbs: 13.4g, protein: 0.5g, sugars: 13g, dietary fiber: 1.5g, sodium:0 potassium: 120mg

Healthy Banana Cookies

Prep time: 15 minutes Cook time: 20 minutes serves: 36

Ingredients

3 ripe bananas

2 cups rolled oats

1cup pitted and chopped dates

1 tbsp vanilla extract

What you'll need from store cupboard

⅓ cup of vegetable oil

Instructions

1. Preheat your oven to 350^0F.

2. In the meantime, mash the bananas in a bowl (large).

3. Add oats, oil, dates, and vanilla then stir to mix well. Let sit for about 15 minutes.

4. Drop onto a cooking sheet (ungreased) by teaspoonful.

5. Bake for about 20 minutes in the oven until browned lightly.

Nutritional Facts per serving

Calories: 56, total fat: 2.4g, saturated fat: 0g, total carbs: 8.4g, net carbs: 7.4g, protein: 0.8g, sugars: 4g, dietary fiber: 1g, sodium: 1mg, potassium: 78mg

Dairy-Free Chocolate Pudding

Prep time: 10 minutes Cook time: 10 minutes serves: 2

Ingredients

3 tbsp cornstarch

¼ tbsp vanilla extract

1½ cups of soy milk

¼ cup of cocoa powder

What you'll need from store cupboard

2 tbsp water

¼ cup white sugar

Instructions

1. Combine water and cornstarch in a small bowl to form a paste.

2. stir together cornstarch mixture, vanilla, soy milk, cocoa, and sugar in a saucepan over medium heat

3. Cook while stirring until mixture boils and thickens then remove from heat. As the mixture cools, the pudding will continue.

4. Allow the mixture to cool for about 5 minutes then place in a refrigerator until it cools completely.

Nutritional facts Per Serving

Calories: 267, total fat: 4.7g, saturated fat: 1g, total carbs: 53.3g, net carbs: 48.5g, protein: 8.1g, sugars: 33g, dietary fiber: 4.8g, sodium: 97mg, potassium: 381mg

Honeydew Sorbet

Prep time: 5 minutes + freeze time Cook time: 0 minutes serves: 4

Ingredients

1 honeydew melon (sliced to 1-inch chunks)

2 tbsp honey or maple syrup

1 tbsp lemon juice

What you'll need from store cupboard

4 tbsp of water

Instructions

1. Spread out the honeydew chunks on a baking sheet then place in the freezer until frozen for about 4-6 hours.

2. Transfer the frozen chunks to a blender (high-powered) then add sweetener and lemon juice.

3. Add water then blend until smooth.

4. Transfer back to the freezer. Freeze for additional 30 minutes until it sets.

5. Scoop, serve, and enjoy.

Nutritional facts per serving

Calories: 124, total fat: 0.5g, saturated fat: 0.2g, total carbs: 31.3g, net carbs: 28.7g, protein: 1.7g, sugars: 28g, sodium: 58mg, potassium: 740mg

Olive Oil Bread

Prep time: 5 minutes Cook time: 10 minutes serves: 2

Ingredients

1 cup all-purpose flour

1 tbsp baking powder

2 tbsp olive oil

Optional: splash of rosemary

What you'll need from store cupboard

½ tbsp salt to taste

⅓ Cup warm water

Instructions

1. Add flour, salt and baking powder in a blender and blend for about 10 seconds.

2. Add water and oil slowly to the blender while still blending. Blend for an additional 30 seconds until dough begins to form.

3. Meanwhile, warm a large skillet (cast-iron) over medium heat then splash olive oil and swirl around to lightly coat the pan.

4. Make 4 small patties from the dough then drop them to the skillet.

5. Cook for about 5 minutes each side.

6. Remove and splash with rosemary.

7. Serve immediately.

Nutritional Facts per Serving

Calories: 163, total fat: 7.8g, saturated fat: 0.9g, total carbs: 22.2g, net carbs: 21.3g, protein: 4g, sugars: 0.1g, dietary fiber: 0.9g, sodium: 292.4mg, potassium: 312mg

Vegetable Mains Recipe

Irish Bombay Potatoes

Prep time: 5 minutes, Cook time: 30 minutes; Serves 4

5 Ingredients

35 oz potato, peeled

2 tbsp curry paste

2 tbsp tomato paste

½ cup basil, fresh

1 garlic clove

What you' ll need from the store cupboard

1tbsp salt

4 tbsp oil

2 tbsp curry powder

2 tbsp white vinegar

Instructions

1. Heat your oven to 390⁰F.

2. Quarter the peeled potatoes and place them in a mixing bowl.

3. Add curry paste, tomato paste, salt, oil, curry powder then mix until the potatoes ate well coated.

4. Layer the potatoes on your oven tray and bake them for fifteen minutes.

5. Add fresh basil and garlic five minutes before the end of cooking. Mix well making sure the spices are well mixed in.

6. Serve with dips or as a side dish. Enjoy.

Nutrition Facts Per Serving

Calories 288, Total Fat 14g, Saturated Fat 1g, Total Carbs 33g, Net Carbs 25g, Protein 7g, Sugar 1g, Fiber 7g, Sodium 670mg, Potassium 1129mg

Healthy Mashed Sweet potato

Prep time: 5 minutes, Cook time: 20 minutes; Serves 2

5 Ingredients

2 sweet potatoes, peeled and chopped

1 chili pepper

2 garlic cloves

1 handful coriander, fresh

1 thumb ginger, fresh

What you'll need from the store cupboard

6 tbsp olive oil

½ juiced lime

Instructions

1. Add sweet potatoes to boiling and salted water in a saucepan. Let the sweet potatoes cook for twenty minutes.

2. Meanwhile, add olive oil to a small pan. Add chopped garlic cloves and ginger.

3. Make an incision on the chili pepper or make four incisions on the chili pepper if you like your food spicier.

4. Let the three fry in oil for some few minutes.

5. When the sweet potatoes are cooked, poke them with a knife to make sure they are fully soft.

6. Add the potatoes in the pan and use a spoon to remove the garlic, ginger and chili pieces from the oil. The heat should be off.

7. Mash all them together until smooth.

8. Serve with coriander and lime juice. Enjoy.

Nutrition Facts Per Serving

Calories 503, Total Fat 42g, Saturated Fat 5g, Total Carbs 31g, Net Carbs 27g, Protein 2g, Sugar 6g, Fiber 4g, Sodium 76mg, Potassium 532mg

Spinach Tomato Quesadilla

Prep time: 5 minutes, Cook time: 10 minutes; Serves 2

5 Ingredients

2 whole-grain tortillas

½ cup cheddar cheese, sliced

1 cup mozzarella cheese, sliced

1 tomato

1 ½ cup spinach

What you' ll need from the store cupboard

1 tbsp homemade pesto

Instructions

1. Spread a layer of homemade pesto over half tortilla.

2. Add a cheese layer on the tortilla.

3. Slice the tomato and a layer on the cheese.

4. Add a layer of spinach on top then finally another cheese layer

5. Fold the other half of the tortilla on top.

6. Place the tortilla on a hot pan, cover the pan and heat for four minutes on each side. The cheese should have melted.

7. Serve and enjoy.

Nutrition Facts Per Serving

Calories 386, Total Fat 19g, Saturated Fat 9g, Total Carbs 26g, Net Carbs 20g, Protein 23g, Sugar 3g, Fiber 5g, Sodium 863mg, Potassium 254mg

Lentil Tacos

Prep time: 5 minutes, Cook time: 15 minutes; Serves 6

5 Ingredients

1 onion, diced

2 garlic cloves, diced

1 cup brown lentils, cooked

2 tbsp burrito seasoning

2 taco shells

What you' ll need from the store cupboard

2 tbsp olive oil

4 cups of water

6 tbsp salsa

1 ½ cups mixed salad

½ cup cherry tomatoes, sliced

Instructions

1. Heat olive oil in a saucepan and fry the onions until soft.

2. Add diced garlic then drain the lentils and add them.

3. Add seasoning and water then stir well. Cook until all water has evaporated.

4. Meanwhile, put the taco shells in the oven to cook for three minutes.

5. Layer the lentils at the bottom followed by cheese if you desire, salsa, mixed salad and finally the cherry tomatoes.

6. Serve and enjoy.

Nutrition Facts Per Serving

Calories 239, Total Fat 13g, Saturated Fat 5g, Total Carbs 20g, Net Carbs 14g, Protein 9g, Sugar 2g, Fiber 5g, Sodium 350mg, Potassium 296mg

Flawless Feta and Spinach Pancakes

Prep time: 10 minutes, Cook time: 20 minutes; Serves 4

5 Ingredients

17 oz spinach, frozen

1 cup flour

2 eggs

1cup milk

5 oz feta cheese

What you' ll need from the store cupboard

2 tbsp butter

Salt to taste

Instructions

1. Heat a pot on medium heat then add the frozen spinach. Stir frequently to deforest the spinach quickly.

2. Add flour, eggs, and milk in a mixing bowl then use a hand mixer to mix until there are no lumps.

3. Add more milk until you achieve the desired consistency.

4. Heat a nonstick skillet over medium heat.

5. Melt butter and pour the mixture on the pan — Fry for four minutes on each side.

6. Layer the pancake on a plate then pour the heated spinach on one half of the pancake.

7. Layer cheese slices on the spinach then fold the pancake.

8. Serve and enjoy.

Nutrition Facts Per Serving

Calories 361, Total Fat 18g, Saturated Fat 10g, Total Carbs 33g, Net Carbs 27g, Protein 17g, Sugar 5g, Fiber 4g, Sodium 593mg, Potassium 583mg

Eggplant Curry

Prep time: 5 minutes, Cook time: 30 minutes; Serves 2

5 Ingredients

1 aubergine

1 red onion

2 garlic cloves, crushed

1 cup tomatoes, chopped

1 ½ cups of coconut milk

What you ' ll need from the store cupboard

2 tbsp olive oil

1 tbsp curry powder

1 tbsp turmeric

1 tbsp coriander

Salt and pepper to taste

1 tbsp sugar

Instructions

1. Cook the rice according to the package directions

2. Fry the aubergine in olive oil over high heat for four minutes. Stir well so that it doesn't burn.

3. Add onions then lower the heat to medium. Cook for five minutes.

4. Stir in garlic, curry powder, turmeric, and coriander — Cook for four minutes.

5. Add tomatoes and milk then season with salt and pepper to taste.

6. Simmer until your desired consistency is achieved.

7. Add sugar for a little sweetener if you desire.

8. Serve and enjoy

Nutrition Facts Per Serving

Calories 379, Total Fat 27g, Saturated Fat 14g, Total Carbs 27g, Net Carbs 17g, Protein 3g, Sugar 10g, Fiber 9g, Sodium 749mg, Potassium 663mg

Pasta, Noodles, And Dumplings Recipe

Dumplings

Prep time: 5 minutes Cook time: 15 minutes; serves 6

Ingredients

1 cup all-purpose flour

1 tbsp white sugar

1 tbsp margarine

½ cup milk

What you'll need from store cupboard

2 tbsp baking powder

½ tbsp salt

Instructions

1. Stir together flour, sugar, baking powder, and salt in a bowl (medium-size).

2. Cut in margarine until crumbly.

3. Add milk and stir to make dough soft.

4. Drop the dough into a boiling stew by spoonfuls then cover and simmer for about 15 minutes. Do not lift lid.

5. Serve.

Nutritional Facts Per Servings

Calories: 105 total fat: 2.4g saturated fat: 1g total carbs: 18g net carbs: 17.4g protein: 2.8g sugars: 2g dietary fiber: 0.6g sodium: 386mg potassium: 54mg

Potato Dumplings II

Prep time: 10 minutes Cook time: 20 minutes; serves 6

Ingredients

1 cup instant mashed potato flakes

1 cup hot water

¾ cup all-purpose flour

What you'll need from store cupboard

1 tbsp salt

2 eggs

Instructions

1. Put potato flakes, salt, and water in a mixing bowl. Mix and allow to cool for about 10 minutes.

2. Add eggs and flour and stir.

3. Knead the dough on a surface (lightly floured) until not sticky. Make 6 dumplings from the dough.

4. Boil water in a large saucepan then drop in the dumplings.

5. Boil for about 20 minutes until dumplings rise to the top.

6. Remove and drain the dumplings.

Nutritional Facts Per Servings

Calories: 108 total fat: 1.9g saturated fat: 1g total carbs: 18.1g net carbs: 17.1g protein: 4.3g sugars: 0g Dietary fiber: 1g sodium: 419mg potassium: 142mg

Grandma's Noodles II

Prep time 2 hours: Cook time: 30 minutes; serves 4

Ingredients

2 tbsp milk

1 cup all-purpose (sifted)

What you'll need from store cupboard

1 beaten egg

½ tbsp salt

Optional: ½ tbsp baking powder

Instructions

1. Combine egg, milk, and salt then add flour and mix. (add baking powder for thicker noodles before mixing).

2. Separate the mixture into two balls.

3. Roll out dough then let sit for about 20 minutes.

4. Cut the dough into strips then spread to dry. Dust with flour and let dry for about 2 hours.

5. Drop the strips into hot soup and cook for about 10 minutes.

6. Serve and enjoy.

Nutritional Facts Per Serving

Calories: 136 total fat: 1.7g saturated fat: 1g total carbs: 24.5g net carbs: 23.7g protein: 5.1g sugars: 1g dietary fiber: 0.8g sodium: 373mg potassium: 62mg

Pasta with Fresh Tomato Sauce

Prep time: 15 minutes Cook time: 10 minutes; serves 8

Ingredients

16 oz dry penne pasta

8 Roma plum tomatoes, diced

¼ cup fresh basil, finely chopped

½ cup Italian dressing

What you'll need from store cupboard

¼ cup parmesan cheese (grated)

¼ cup red onion (diced)

Salt to taste

Instructions

1. Boil lightly salted water in a large pot then add penne pasta and cook for about 10 minutes until al dente. Now drain.

2. Transfer the cooked pasta into a large bowl and toss with tomatoes, basil, Italian dressing, parmesan cheese, and red onion.

3. Serve and enjoy.

Nutrition Facts Per Serving

Calories: 257 total fat: 3.1g saturated fat: 1g total carbs: 46.9g net carbs: 43.5g protein: 9.8g sugars: 3g dietary fiber: 3.4g sodium: 248mg potassium: 236mg

Penne with Spring Vegetables

Prep time: 10 minutes Cook time: 15 minutes; Serves 4

Ingredients

1 lb trimmed fresh asparagus (½ inch pieces)

8 oz trimmed sugar snap peas

8 oz dry penne pasta

What you'll need from store cupboard

½ cup parmesan cheese (grated)

3 tbsp olive oil

Pepper and salt to taste

Instructions

1. Boil lightly salted water in a large pot then add asparagus and cook for about 2 minutes.

2. Add peas and cook for an additional 2 minutes. Transfer to a set-aside bowl (large).

3. Add pasta to the boiling water then cook for about 8-10 minutes until al dente. Now drain.

4. Add pasta to the bowl with asparagus then toss with parmesan, olive oil, pepper, and salt.

5. Serve.

Nutritional Facts per Serving

Calories: 383 total fat: 14.4g saturated fat: 3g total carbs: 50.4g net carbs: 44.8g Protein: 15.2g sugars: 4g dietary fiber: 5.6g sodium: 158mg potassium: 347mg

Rice And Grains Recipe

One Pan Mexican Rice

Prep time: 10 minutes, Cook time: 30 minutes; Serves 6

5 Ingredients

1 cup brown rice, quick cook

1 can kidney beans drain and rinse

1 can corn, drained

What you ' ll need from the store cupboard

1 ½ cup water

½ tbsp oregano, dried

½ tbsp salt

⅛ tbsp black pepper

1 can tomato sauce

1 tbsp adobo seasoning

1 tbsp cumin

1 tbsp garlic powder

1 tbsp onion powder

Instructions

1. Add all the ingredients to a nonstick skillet.

2. Bring to boil.

3. Reduce heat to medium and cover the skillet. Simmer until the rice is soft and all the liquid is absorbed.

4. Remove the lid and reduce heat to low. Stir occasionally until the rice is completely cooked.

5. Serve and enjoy.

Nutrition Facts Per Serving

Calories 153, Total Fat 1g, Saturated Fat 0g, Total Carbs 33g, Net Carbs 28g, Protein 5g, Sugar 7g, Fiber 3g, Sodium 794mg, Potassium 542 mg

Red Rice and Beans

Prep time: 10 minutes, Cook time: 60 minutes; Serves 6

5 Ingredients

¼ tbsp red pepper flakes

1 can tomatoes, diced

2 cups brown rice, long grain

1 can black beans, rinsed

¼ cup cilantro

What you ' ll need from the store cupboard

¼ cup extra virgin oil

1 onion, diced

1 bell pepper, diced

2 garlic cloves

1 tbsp cumin, ground

4 cups vegetable broth

Instructions

1. Add oil in your heavy-bottomed skillet then sauté onions for three minutes.

2. Add bell pepper and sauté for four minutes.

3. Add garlic, ground cumin, and pepper flakes. Sauté for a minute.

4. Add tomatoes and stir cook for five minutes.

5. Add brown rice and vegetable broth then stir to mix everything. Bring to boil then reduce heat to low. Simmer until the brown rice is cooked through.

6. Stir in cilantro and beans then let rest for five minutes.

7. Serve and enjoy

Nutrition Facts Per Serving

Calories 445, Total Fat 11g, Saturated Fat 1g, Total Carbs 74g, Net Carbs 62g, Protein 12g, Sugar 1g, Fiber 5g, Sodium 645mg, Potassium 617mg

Mexican Brown Rice

Prep time: 10 minutes, Cook time: 10 minutes; Serves 5

5 Ingredients

1 ½ cups corn, fresh

1 can black beans, drain and rinse

3 cups brown rice, whole grain and ready to serve

1 cup jarred salsa

Cilantro for garnish

What you ' ll need from the store cupboard

1 tbsp chili powder

Instructions

1.   Preheat your nonstick skillet over medium heat.

2.   Add corn and beans then cook until tender.

3.   Add rice and chili powder then stir to combine. Stir cook for three minutes.

4.   Stir in jarred salsa and cook until everything is warmed through.

5.   Remove from heat and let rest for ten minutes. Garnish with cilantro.

6.   Serve and enjoy.

Nutrition Facts Per Serving

Calories 215, Total Fat 3g, Saturated Fat 1g, Total Carbs 42g, Net Carbs 35g, Protein 8g, Sugar 2g, Fiber 7g, Sodium 458mg, Potassium 417mg

Black Beans and Rice

Prep time: 5 minutes, Cook time: 30 minutes; Serves 10

5 Ingredients

1 onion, chopped

2 garlic cloves, minced

¾ cup white rice

1 /4 tbsp cayenne pepper

3 ½ cups black beans, canned, drained and rinsed

What you ' ll need from the store cupboard

1 tbsp olive oil

1 ½ cup vegetable broth, low sodium, and low fat

1 tbsp cumin, ground

Instructions

1. Add olive oil in a stockpot over medium heat. Add onions and garlic. Saute for four minutes.

2. Add rice and saute for two more minutes.

3. Add vegetable broth and bring to boil. Cover, lower heat to medium and cook for twenty more minutes.

4. Add cumin, cayenne pepper, and black beans then stir.

5. Serve and enjoy

Nutrition Facts Per Serving

Calories 140, Total Fat 1g, Saturated Fat 0g, Total Carbs 27g, Net Carbs 19g, Protein 6g, Sugar 1g, Fiber 6g, Sodium 354mg, Potassium 298mg

Coconut Rice with Black Beans

Prep time: 5 minutes, Cook time: 25 minutes; Serves 6

5 Ingredients

½ shallot, minced

1 cup jasmine rice, uncooked

¾ cup coconut milk

1 pinch nutmeg, ground

1 can black beans, drained and rinsed

What you ' ll need from the store cupboard

1 tbsp butter

1 cup water

Instructions

1. Melt butter in a saucepan over medium-high heat. Sauté until the shallots are translucent.

2. Add jasmine rice and stir until the rice is evenly coated with melted butter.

3. Add coconut milk and water. Season with nutmeg then bring to boil over high heat.

4. Reduce to medium and simmer until rice is tender, and there is no liquid.

5. Stir in the beans and cook until hot.

6. Serve and enjoy.

Nutrition Facts Per Serving

Calories 190, Total Fat 8g, Saturated Fat 7g, Total Carbs 27g, Net Carbs 25g, Protein 3g, Sugar 0g, Fiber 1g, Sodium 19mg, Potassium 78mg

Quick Black Beans and Rice

Prep time: 5 minutes, Cook time: 15 minutes; Serves 6

5 Ingredients

1 onion, chopped

1 can black beans, undrained

1 can stewed tomatoes

1 tbsp oregano, dried

1 ½ brown rice, uncooked

What you ' ll need from the store cupboard

1 tbsp vegetable oil

½ tbsp garlic powder

Instructions

1. Heat vegetable oil in a large saucepan over medium heat.

2. Add onion and sauté until tender.

3. Add beans, stewed tomatoes, dried oregano, and garlic. Bring to boil.

4. Stir in brown rice, reduce heat to low. Simmer for five minutes and remove from heat.

5. Let rest for five minutes then serve. Enjoy.

Nutrition Facts Per Serving

Calories 271, Total Fat 5g, Saturated Fat 0g, Total Carbs 48g, Net Carbs 35g, Protein 10g, Sugar 5g, Fiber 9g, Sodium 552mg, Potassium 260mg

Mashed Green Soybeans

Prep time: 5 minutes Cook time: 35 minutes serves: 4

Ingredients

12 oz shelled green soybeans (frozen)

2 smashed and peeled garlic cloves

Water to cover

What you'll need from store cupboard

½ tbsp kosher salt

½ tbsp black pepper (freshly ground)

3 tbsp olive oil (extra-virgin)

Instructions

1. Combine soybeans, salt, and garlic in a saucepan then add water to cover them completely.

2. Cook for about 30 minutes on low boil then drain the liquid.

3. Transfer soybeans and garlic to a blender then season with black pepper.

4. Blend on high while adding olive oil until smooth.

Nutritional facts per serving

Calories: 219 total fat: 15.9g saturated fat: 2g total carbs: 10.1g net carbs: 6.4g protein: 11.1g sugars: 0g fiber: 3.7g sodium: 255mg potassium: 537mg

Simple Roasted Soybeans

Prep time: 5 minutes Cook time: 20 minutes serves: 6

Ingredients

12 oz frozen soybeans (in their pods)

2 minced garlic cloves

What you'll need from store cupboard

2 tbsp olive oil (extra-virgin)

1 tbsp sea salt

½ tbsp black pepper (ground)

Instructions

1. Preheat your oven to 375^0F.

2. Add soybeans, garlic, olive oil, salt and pepper in a bowl (large). Toss together until well-coated.

3. Spread the mixture on a baking sheet in a single layer.

4. Roast in the oven for about 20 minutes until soybeans shells begin to brown. Stir half-way through.

5. Serve whole. Pop bens out to eat.

Nutritional Facts Per Serving

Calories: 126 total fat: 8.4g saturated fat: 1g total carbs: 6.7g net carbs: 4.3g protein: 7.4g sugars: 0g fiber: 2.4g sodium: 302mg potassium: 360mg

Quick and Easy Refried Beans

Prep time: 10 minutes Cook time: 10 minutes serves: 6

Ingredients

2 peeled garlic cloves

15 oz pinto beans

1 tbsp chili powder

1 tbsp cumin

½ lime (juiced)

What you'll need from store cupboard

2 tbsp canola oil

Salt to taste

Instructions

1. Heat oil in a skillet (heavy) on medium heat.

2. Add garlic cloves and cook for about 4-5 minutes until browned on both sides. Turn once.

3. Smash the cloves using a fork while in the skillet.

4. Add beans, chili powder, cumin and salt then cook for about 5 minutes until beans are heated thoroughly. Make sure to stir occasionally.

5. Smash the mixture using a potato masher until desired texture.

6. Pour over the lime juice and stir to combine.

7. Serve and enjoy.

Nutritional information

Calories: 132 total fat: 5.6g saturated fat: 1g total carbs: 16.1g net carbs: 11.3g protein: 5g sugars: 0g dietary fiber: 4.8g sodium: 323mg potassium: 265mg

Buttery Garlic Green Beans

Prep time: 10 minutes Cook time: 10 minutes serves: 4

Ingredients

1lb fresh green beans (trimmed and half snapped)

3 minced garlic cloves

2 pinches lemon pepper

What you'll need from store cupboard

3 tbsp butter

Salt to taste

Instructions

1. Place beans in a skillet (large) and cover with water. Boil over medium-high heat.

2. Reduce to medium-low heat then simmer for about 5 minutes until beans begin to soften.

3. Drain water then add butter. Cook for about 2-3 minutes while stirring until butter melts.

4. Add garlic and cook for about 4-5 minutes until garlic is fragrant and tender.

5. Season with salt and lemon pepper.

6. Serve.

Nutritional facts per serving

Calories: 116 total fat: 8.8g saturated fat: 6.0g total carbs: 8.9g net carbs: 5g protein: 2.3g sugars: 2g dietary fiber: 3.9g sodium: 222mg potassium: 250mg

Best Green Bean Casserole

Prep time: 10 minutes Cook time: 15 minutes serves: 6

Ingredients

11 oz condensed cream (from mushroom soup)

15 oz drained green beans

What you'll need from store cupboard

1 cup cheddar cheese (shredded)

6 oz onions (French fried)

Instructions

1. Preheat your oven to 350^0F.

2. Meanwhile, place soup and beans in a large bowl (microwave-safe) and mix well.

3. Microwave on high for about 3-5 minutes until warm.

4. Add ½ cup cheese, stir and microwave for additional 2-3 minutes.

5. Transfer the mixture to dish (casserole) the splash with onions and cheese remainder.

6. Place in the oven and bake until onion starts to brown and cheese melts.

7. Serve and enjoy.

Nutritional Facts Per Serving

Calories: 322 total fat: 23.2g saturated fat: 9g total carbs: 20.2mg net carbs: 17.9g protein: 6.6g sugars: 3g dietary fiber: 2.3g sodium: 1068mg potassium: 50mg

Extra Easy Hummus

Prep time: 5 minutes Cook time: 0 minutes servings: 4

Ingredients

1 can (15-ounce) drained garbanzo beans (liquid reserved)

2 tbsp ground cumin

1 crushed garlic cloves

What you'll need from store cupboard

1 tbsp olive oil

½ tbsp salt

Instructions

1. Combine beans, salt, cumin, garlic and olive oil in a blender.

2. Blend on low adding reserved liquid gradually until the consistency of your liking.

3. Serve.

Nutritional Facts Per Serving

Calories: 118 total fat: 4.4g saturated fat: 1g total carbs: 16.5g net carbs: 13.3g protein: 3.7g sugars:0g dietary fiber: 3.2g sodium: 502mg potassium: 142mg

Savory Flat Breads, Pizza, Tarts And More Recipe

Tomato Tart

Prep time: 30 minutes, Cook time: 30 minutes; Serves 4

5 Ingredients

4 tbsp cheese, soft

Olives for decorate

1 tbsp Dijon mustard

Chunk parmesan

1 lb. puff pastry

What you'll need from the store cupboard

8 ripe tomatoes, sliced

Flour for rolling out

Instructions

1. Preheat your oven to 395⁰F.

2. Mix the cheese with dijon mustard in a mixing bowl.

3. Roll the pastry on a floured surface into a rectangle.

4. Place the rectangle pastry on a baking sheet. Trim wiggy edges.

5. Mark an even border around the pastry edges then spread cheese inside the border.

6. Arrange tomato on the cheese then garnish with olives.

7. Spread grated parmesan all over.

8. Place the tart in your preheated oven to bake until the pastry is golden brown.

9. Remove from oven, let cool and serve. Enjoy.

Nutrition Facts Per Serving

Calories 508, Total Fat 38g, Saturated Fat 19g, Total Carbs 34g, Net Carbs 30g, Protein 10g, Sugar 3g, Fiber 3g, Sodium 328mg, Potassium 442 mg

Puff Pizza Tart

Prep time: 5 minutes, Cook time: 20 minutes; Serves 4

5 Ingredients

1 lb sheet puff pastry, ready rolled

5 tbsp red pesto

2 oz salami, sliced

4 oz ball mozzarella, pieces

Handful rocket

What you'll need from the store cupboard

Extra virgin oil

Salt and pepper to taste

Instructions

1. Preheat oven to 400^0F.

2. Unroll the puff pastry on a baking sheet and use a fork prick its surface.

3. Mark a border around the edges of the pastry then spread the red pesto inside the border.

4. Layer the sliced salami and mozzarella on the pesto.

5. Season to taste then bake until the pastry is golden brown.

6. Drizzle olive oil and scatter a handful of rockets. Serve and enjoy.

Nutrition Facts Per Serving

Calories 597, Total Fat 47g, Saturated Fat 19g, Total Carbs 26g, Net Carbs 24g, Protein 18g, Sugar 1g, Fiber 1g, Sodium 271mg, Potassium 154 mg

Veggie Pizza

Prep time: 15 minutes, Cook time: 25 minutes; Serves 5

5 Ingredients

1 lb carton passata

5 large flatbreads

1 garlic clove

3 balls mozzarella, pat dry and tore into pieces

Nutmeg, freshly grated

What you ' ll need from the store cupboard

1 lb spinach frozen, deforested

5 eggs

2 tbsp basil

Instructions

1. Preheat your oven to the highest level of hotness.

2. Meanwhile, spread passata on each flat-bread.

3. Squeeze water from spinach then scatters them on top of the passata leaving a space at the center.

4. Divide garlic and mozzarella among the flatbreads. Put two pizzas on a baking tray and crack an egg into the space at the center of each pizza.

5. Season with nutmeg and basil as you desire.

6. Bake until the egg is cooked and the cheese has melted.

7. Repeat the process with all the pizzas.

8. Cut into pieces and serve. Enjoy.

Nutrition Facts Per Serving

Calories 444, Total Fat 22g, Saturated Fat 12g, Total Carbs 36g, Net Carbs 31g, Protein 28g, Sugar 5g, Fiber 4g, Sodium 700mg, Potassium 242 mg

Seeded Flatbreads

Prep time: 45 minutes, Cook time: 30 minutes; Serves 12

5 Ingredients

0.5 oz sachet yeast, dried

14 oz white bread flour

7 oz whole meal bread flour

1 tbsp black onion seeds

2 tbsp sesame seeds

What you ' ll need from the store cupboard

1 tbsp Caster sugar

2 tbsp oil

Salt to taste

Instructions

1. Mix the dried yeast with two tablespoons of water and caster sugar. Let rest for a few minutes.
2. Tip both flours in a mixing bowl and add a tablespoon of salt.mix well.
3. Add the yeast mixture with a half litre of warm water into the mixing bowl.
4. Mix well with a wooden spoon.
5. Tip the dough on a work surface and knead until elastic and smooth.
6. Oil a bowl and place the dough in it. Cover with a towel and leave it in a warm place.
7. Let it rise until dough doubles its size.
8. Knock out all the air in the dough then knead in the seeds. Make sure they are evenly distributed.
9. Divide the dough into twelve equal pieces and roll out each piece as thinly as you can.
10. Cook the flatbreads in a nonstick skillet until both sides are well cooked, and bubbles appear.
11. Wrap the flatbreads in a foil and store.

Nutrition Facts Per Serving

Calories 189, Total Fat 3g, Saturated Fat 0g, Total Carbs 34g, Net Carbs 31g, Protein 7g, Sugar 1g, Fiber 3g, Sodium 0 mg, Potassium 0 mg

Roasted Veggie Flatbread

Prep time: 20 minutes, Cook time: 25 minutes; Serves 12 slices

5 Ingredients

16 oz pizza dough

6 oz goat cheese, divided

¾ cup parmesan cheese, divided

3 tbsp fresh dill, divided

1 red pepper, sliced

What you' ll need from the store cupboard

1 red onion

1 zucchini

2 tomatoes

1 tbsp olive oil

Salt to taste

Instructions

1. Preheat oven to 400^0F

2. Roll the pizza dough into a rectangle.

3. Spray a parchment paper with nonstick spray and place the dough on it.

4. Spread half the goat cheese on half the pizza dough.

5. Sprinkle half parmesan cheese and half the dill.

6. Fold the other half of the dough carefully over the cheese. Sprinkle the remaining goat cheese and parmesan cheese.

7. Layer the vegetables on the cheese creating your desired pretty pattern.

8. Brush oil and season with salt, pepper, and dill to taste.

9. Bake until the edges are golden brown. Cut into two-inch slices and serve when warm.

Nutrition Facts Per Serving

Calories 170, Total Fat 6g, Saturated Fat 3g, Total Carbs 21g, Net Carbs 19g, Protein 8g, Sugar 4g, Fiber 1g, Sodium 424mg, Potassium 137 mg

Dilly Veggie Pizza

Prep time: 20 minutes, Cook time: 10 minutes; Serves 15

5 Ingredients

8 oz refrigerated crescent rolls

1 cup vegetable dill dip

1 cup fresh broccoli

1 cup chopped tomatoes, seeded

1 can ripe olives, drained and sliced

What you' ll need from the store cupboard

2 carrots, chopped

4 onions, sliced

Instructions

1. Preheat your oven to 375^0F

2. Unroll the crescent rolls into a rectangle.

3. Grease a baking pan then press the dough on it. Make sure you seal the seams.

4. Bake until golden brown then cool completely.

5. Spread the dill dip on the crust then sprinkle broccoli, tomatoes, olives, carrots, and onions.

6. Cut into squares. Serve and enjoy.

7. Leftovers can be refrigerated.

Nutrition Facts Per Serving

Calories 225, Total Fat 20g, Saturated Fat 3g, Total Carbs 11g, Net Carbs 9g, Protein 2g, Sugar 3g, Fiber 1g, Sodium 290mg, Potassium 325 mg

Sandwiches, Wraps, Burgers And More Recipe

Salmon Burgers

Prep time: 10 minutes, Cook time: 4 minutes; serves 4

5 Ingredients

¾ cup dated oats

1 tbsp minced garlic

6 oz can feral Alaskan salmon

1 egg

½ diced yellow onions

What you'll need from the cupboard

Salt to taste

Pepper to taste

Cooking spray

Instructions

1. Add oats in a food processor then consistency pulse into flour-like

2. Add in Alaska salmon, diced yellow onions, garlic, egg, salt, and pepper. Stir to combine the mixture until it forms paste-like consistency. Scrape the sides a few times.

3. Divide into 4 patties then place them into the fridge and wait for 15-20 minutes.

4. When ready, heat the pan over medium to high and spray it with cooking spray. Put the patties in a pan and allow to cook for 3 - 4 minutes on each side.

5. You can enjoy as is, or put stuff in between two buns for a perfect taste.

Nutrition per serving

Calories 140, Total fat 3g, saturated fat 0.7g, Total carbs 21.7g, Net carbs 18.5g, Protein 5.3g, Sugar 0g, Fiber 3.2g, sodium 56mg, Potassium 167mg.

Blt Wraps Recipe

Prep time: 10 minutes, Cook time: 15minutes, serves 4

5 Ingredients

1 lb thick sliced bacon

½ head iceberg lettuce striped

½ lb of grape or cherry tomatoes, halved

¼ cup mayonnaise sauce or ranch dressing

4 tortillas bread flour

What you'll need from the cupboard

Salt and Pepper to taste

Instructions

1. Place a large pan with bacon strips over medium-low heat, cook slowly until the desired crispness is achieved.

2. Place the iceberg lettuce in a mixing bowl. Slice tomatoes in half and mix with stripped lettuce .dice the striped bacon pieces and toss in a bowl to combine with tomatoes and lettuce.

3. Add ranch dressing or mayo sauce to the bowl and mix until all ingredients are evenly coated. Relish with salt and pepper to taste.

4. Place a cup of filling in the center of tortilla flour. Bend both sides into the center and roll it closed like a burrito. (to keep the wraps closed you can use a toothpick or wrap with parchment)

5. Serve immediately.

Nutrition per serving

Calories 852, Total fat 57g Saturated fat 16g, Total carbs 43g, Net carbs 42g, Protein 44g, Sugar 5g, Fiber 1g, Sodium 2880mg, Potassium 203mg.

Finger Cucumber Sandwiches

Prep time: 20 minutes, Cook time: 0 minutes serves: 20

Ingredients

1 Cup English cucumber stripped

8 oz cream cheese

4 tbsp sour cream

½ tbsp dill, chopped

1 tbsp. Green onion, chopped

What you'll need from the cupboard

10 slices of bread

¼ tbsp salt

Instructions

1. In a bowl combine striped cucumber and salt. Wait for 10 minutes.

2. In another bowl combine soured cream, cream cheese, green onion, dill, mix well.

3. Drain the excess water from the cucumber after 10 minutes by just squeezing it. Get rid of the water.

4. Combine cucumber and cream cheese mixture and mix well.

5. Prepare 5 slices of bread, spread cucumber cream cheese mixture about 3 tbsp on each slice.

6. Cover with the remaining slices of bread. Cut into four equal pieces.

Nutrition per serving

Calories 58, Total fat 4.6g, saturated fat 2.8g, Total carbs 2.9g, Net carbs 2.7g, Proteins 1.3g,Sugar 0g, Fiber 0.2g, Sodium 97mg, Potassium 33g.

Salmon Burger

Prep time: 5minutes Cook time: 10 minutes serves 4

Ingredients

⅔ Cup butter beans

¾ lb fresh salmon (chunks)

¼ tbsp pepper (each and salt)

1 avocado in slices

4 wheat buns (hamburger buns)

What you'll need from the cupboard

1 tbsp olive oil

Instructions

1. Add together butter beans, salmon, pepper, and salt in a food processor, blend till salmon mixture is obtained. This process should take a few seconds.

2. Put 1 tbsp of olive oil in a frying pan and heat over medium heat.

3. Form 4 burger patties from the mixture and place them in the already hot pan, cook for 4 minutes each side. At this point, the burger reaches internal temperature of 145 F.

4. Top each salmon burger on a bun with sliced avocado.

Nutrition per serving (1 Serving is: - 1Patty, ¼ Avocado and 1 bun)

Calories 371,Total Fat 20.5g,Saturated Fat 3.7g ,Total Carbs28.2g,Net Carbs20.7g,Protein22.4g,Sugar:3.7g,Fiber:7.5g,Sodium:171mg,Potassium 795mg

Roasted Veggies & Hummus Sandwich

Prep time: 10 Minutes; Cook time: 35 minutes; Serves 1

Ingredients

½ cup sliced vegetables (eggplant, bell peppers and summer squash)

1 slice whole wheat bread

2 tbsp hummus

½ cup spinach leaves

1 tbsp sunflower seeds, raw & unsalted

What you'll need from the store/cupboard

1 tbsp olive oil

Instructions

1. Preheat oven to 350^0F.

2. Disseminate sliced vegetables on a small edged flat pan, add Olive oil and roast for about 25 minutes till tender.

3. Toast the bread slice if you desire.

4. Lay hummus on the slice of bread and top with spinach. Add the roasted vegetables on top of the spinach then spread sunflower seeds.

Nutrition per serving

Calories 300,Total Fat 19.5g, Saturated Fat 2.8g,Total Carbs 25.4g,Net Carbs 16.6g,Protein 8.6g,Sugar:1.7g,Fiber 8.8g,Sodium:525mg,Potassium:405mg

Super Vegetable Wrap

Prep time: 5 Minutes; Cook time: 0 minutes; Serves 1

Ingredients

2 tbsp carrot, grated

¼ cup cheddar cheese, Shredded

2 tbsp Tomatoes, Fragmented

2 wheat tortillas

¼ cup grated lettuce

What you'll need from the store/cupboard

1 tbsp KRAFT ranch dressing, classic

Preparation Instructions

1. Assemble carrots, ranch dressing, cheddar cheese and tomatoes in a dish and mix.

2. On top of the wheat tortilla, spread half of the obtained mixture and add 2 tbsp of lettuce.

3. Roll up the tortilla and wrap it in cling wrap.

Nutrition per serving

Calories 294,Total fat 24.3g,Saturated fat 12.7g,Total carbs 4.4g, Net carbs 3.7g,Protein 14.4g,Sugar:2.2g,Fiber:0.7g,Sodium:492mg,Potassium:172mg

Eggs For Breakfast And Dinners Recipe

Spinach with Fried Eggs

Prep Time: 10 Minutes; Cook time: 25 Minutes; Serves 4

Ingredients

1 Onion chopped

1 lb spinach, cleaned and chopped roughly

Salt to taste

Ground black pepper to taste

4 eggs

What you'll need from the store cupboard

2 tbsp olive oil

Instructions

1. In a large frying pan, add olive oil and heat over medium heat. Add in diced onion and cook for about five minutes.

2. Add spinach then spice with salt and ground black pepper. Cook till the spinach sags and becomes tender.

3. Sink some 4 small reservoirs in the spinach mixture and break an egg on each reservoir. Cook for about 4 minutes until the eggs turn white.

4. Spay black pepper and salt on each egg.

5. Serve while hot.

Nutrition Facts Per Serving

Calories 161,Total fat 11.9g, Saturated fat 2.4g, Total carbs 7.4g,Net carbs 4.2g,Protein 9.1g,Sugars:2g,Fiber: 3.2g,Sodium: 346mg,Potassium

Green Bagel Topped With Poached Eggs

Prep time: 5 minutes; Cook time: 5minutes; Serves 2

Ingredients

1 seeded wholemeal bagel, halved

½ avocado, ripe

¼ lemon slice

1 egg

What you' ll need from the store cupboard

Black pepper to taste

Salt to taste

Instructions

1. Boil 5ml of water in a skillet and toast the bagel while the water boils.

2. Mix black pepper, salt, and avocado in a mixing bowl. Mash until smooth. Squeeze in the lemon slice.

3. Crack the egg in a small plate and put it into the boiling water. Cook for three minutes then lower heat to simmer.

4. Meanwhile, spread the avocado mixture onto the two bagel halves. Place them on warm saucers.

5. Using a chopstick, remove the egg from the boiling water and drain it. Put on top of the bagels and then serve.

Nutrition information per serving

Calories 274,Total fat 13.2g, Saturated fat 3g, Total carbs 33.2g,Net carbs 24.8g,Protein 9.8g,Sugar:11.6g,Fiber:8.4g,Sodium:179mg,Potassium:1170mg

Egg and Honey Toast

Prep time: 5minutes; Cook time: 4minutes; Serves: 2

Ingredients

2 eggs

2 tbsp honey, clear

2 bread slices, Wholemeal

3 oz berries

What you ' ll need from the store cupboard

Cooking spray oil

Yogurt cheese

Instructions

1. Crack the eggs in a small dish and mix with honey. Soak one of the bread slices till it absorbs the egg.

2. Add cooking spray oil in a non-stick pan and heat. Place the egg-soaked bread slice on the hot pan and cook for two minutes. Flip the other side using a spatula, cook further for 2 minutes. Remove from the pan and place on a plate. Repeat the process with the other bread slice

3. Cut the bread into two halves, top with honey, yogurt cheese and mixed berries and serve.

Nutrition information per serving

Calories 244,Total fat 7.5g, Saturated fat 3.3g, Total carbs 26.7g,Net carbs 26.4g,Protein 18.5g,Sugar:22.5g,Fiber:0.3g,Sodium:169mg,Potassium:247mg

Baked Rotini Recipe

Prep time: 10 minutes Cook time: 30minutes Serves: 8

Ingredients

16 oz whole wheat rotini noodles

½ cup pasta (reserved liquid)

17 oz jarred spaghetti sauce

2 cups soft white cheese

2 cups mozzarella cheese, shredded

What you'll need from the cupboard

1 egg, whisked

Instructions

1. Preheat roaster to 350^{0}F

2. Cook pasta 2 minutes less than the package directions in salty boiling water. Drain it reserving ½ of cooking liquid.

3. Mix reserved sauce together with cooked pasta, soft white cheese, egg, sauce and 1 cup cheese shreds.

4. Pour mixture into large cooking vessel 9x13 or casserole dish and top with the remaining white cheese.

5. Bake until cheese is fizzy, or for 30 minutes.

6. You can prepare earlier up to baking, and if coming from the fridge add 20 minutes to the baking time.

Nutrition information per serving

Calories 685, Total fat 13.2g, Saturated fat 7.2g, Total carbs 109.1g, Net carbs 102.1g, Protein 26.4g, Sugar 26.4, Fiber 7g, Sodium 7160mg, Potassium 840mg.

Vegetarian Meatballs

Prep time: 15 minutes Cook time: 15 minutes; serves 10

5 Ingredients

3 cups cauliflower about 1 head.

3 cups brown rice and / or cooked quinoa

¾ cups oat flour, breadcrumbs or almond meal

4 eggs

1 tbsp spices (paprika, chili powder and / or cumin)

What you'll need from the cupboard

2 tbsp salt

3 tbsp olive oil

Instructions

1. Put cauliflower florets in a bowl of boiling water for about 5 minutes, until fork-tender. And drain.

2. Blend cauliflower and quinoa until semi-smooth transfer the mixture into a large bowl and mix with all other ingredients, mix until everything is incorporated. Measure about 1 piled up tablespoon and roll into balls.

3. Put a thin layer of olive oil in a cooking pot and heat over medium heat.

4. Add the balls and cook gently for a few minutes turning every side often to get browned all around.

5. Serve with sauces, salad or freeze for later.

Nutritional facts

Calories: 134, Total fat 7.6g, saturated fat 0.5g, Total carbs 12.2g, Net carbs 7.2g, protein 5g sugar 1.1g, fiber 5g, sodium 442.8mg, potassium 212mg.

Impossibly Easy Spinach And Feta Pie Recipe

Prep time: 10 minutes Cook time: 40 minutes; serves 6.

5 Ingredients

10 oz chopped spinach (frozen) defrosted and squeezed to drain

½ cup feta cheese, crushed

4 sliced green onions

½ cup reduced-fat baking mix or original Bisquick.

2 eggs

What you'll need from the cupboard

⅔ Cup milk

¼ tbsp salt

⅛ tbsp pepper.

Instructions

1. Heat skillet up to 400^0 F grease pie pan 9x1 ¼ inches. Mix spinach, onions, and cheese in a pan.

2. Mix remaining ingredients in a bowl until blended and pour into pie pan.

3. Cook 30 to 35 minutes or test by inserting a knife in the center and comes out clean.

4. Let rest for 5 minutes before serving.

Nutritional information

Calories 123 Total Fat 6.3, saturated fat 3.1, Total carbs 10.5g, Net carbs 9g, Protein 6.8, Sugar 3.4g, Fiber 1.5g, Sodium 624mg, Potassium 351mg.

5-Ingredient Salt and Vinegar Kale Chips

Prep time: 5 minutes Cook time: 25 minutes serves: 4

Ingredients

1 tbsp white vinegar

5 oz kale (stem removed and cut into pieces)

3 tbsp nutritional yeast (divided)

What you'll need from store cupboard

1 tbsp olive oil

¼ tbsp sea salt

Instructions

1. Preheat oven to 300^0F. Use silicone mats to Line 2 baking sheets.

2. Meanwhile, whisk together white vinegar and olive oil in a bowl (large).

3. Add kale pieces then massage with vinegar mixture.

4. Add ⅔ tbsp nutritional yeast and ¼ tbsp salt. Stir and mix to evenly disperse.

5. Arrange on baking sheets in a single layer then splash on top with remaining yeast.

6. Bake for about 20-25 minutes until crispy. Rotate halfway through.

7. Serve.

Nutritional Facts per Serving

Calories: 70, total fat: 4g, saturated fat: 0.6g, total carbs: 5g, net carbs: 3g, protein: 5g, sugar: 0g, dietary fiber: 2g, sodium: 371mg, potassium: 357mg

Chocolate Hummus

Prep time: 5 minutes Cook time: minutes serves: 2

Ingredients

19 oz chickpeas, drained and rinsed

¼ cup raw cacao powder

1 tbsp vanilla extract, pure

What you'll need from store cupboard

¼ cup water

½ tbsp sea salt

Instructions

1. Place all ingredients in a blender (high-speed) then mix until creamy and smooth.

2. Scoop the blended mixture to a bowl. Can be stored in a refrigerator for up to a week.

3. Enjoy as a spread or as a dip.

Nutritional Facts per Serving

Calories: 79 total fat: 1.2g, saturated fat: 0.8g, total carbs: 15.6g, net carbs: 12.3g, protein: 3.3g, sugars: 6.4g, dietary fiber: 3.3g sodium: 120mg potassium: 102mg

Curried Sweet Potato + Carrot Fritters

Prep time: 10 minutes Cook time: 10 minutes; serves 10

Ingredients

1½ cups sweet potato (shredded)

⅓ Cup quinoa flour

1 cup grated carrot

2 tbsp curry powder

What you'll need from store cupboard

1 egg, lightly beaten

Pepper and salt to taste

Coconut oil

Instructions

1. Combine sweet potato, quinoa flour, carrots, beaten egg, curry powder, pepper and salt in a bowl (large). Stir the mixture using a wooden spoon until well combined.

2. Heat about 2-3 tbsp coconut oil into a skillet (large) over medium-high heat.

3. Meanwhile, use your hands to form small patties from the sweet potato mixture.

4. Once the oil is hot, add the fritters and cook for about 2-3 minutes until golden brown. Flip and cook for another 2 minutes.

5. Transfer to a cooling rack.

6. Serve the fritters while slightly warm.

Nutritional Facts per Servings

Calories: 70, total fat: 3g, saturated fat: 2g, total carbs: 8g, net carbs: 7g, protein: 1g, sugars: 1g, fiber: 1g, sodium: 58mg, potassium: 126mg

Healthy Zucchini Fritters

Prep time: 10 minutes Cook time: 10 minutes; serves 12

Ingredients

3½ cups shredded zucchini

½ cup quinoa flour

½ cup chopped scallions

What you'll need from store cupboard

2 large eggs, lightly beaten

Pepper and salt to taste

Coconut oil

Instructions

1. Squeeze all zucchini water using a clean dish towel then transfer to a bowl.

2. Add quinoa flour, eggs, scallions, pepper and salt to the bowl and stir with a wooden spoon until well combined.

3. Heat about 2-3 tbsp coconut oil into a skillet (large) over medium-high heat.

4. Meanwhile, use your hands to form small patties from the zucchini mixture.

5. Once the oil is hot, add the fritters and cook for about 2-3 minutes until golden brown. Flip and cook for another 2 minutes.

6. Repeat for the remaining mixture.

7. Serve warm (slightly). You can also serve with a sauce of your liking.

Nutritional Facts per Serving

Calories: 37, total fat: 1g, saturated fat: 0.3g, total carbs: 4g, net carbs: 2.3g, protein: 2g, sugars: 1g dietary fiber: 1.7g, sodium: 16mg, potassium: 117mg

4-ingredient Snack Mix (Crack Snack)

Prep time: 5 minutes Cook time: 16 minutes

Ingredients

6 oz pecans (chopped)

12 oz Crispix cereal

1 cup salted butter

What you'll need from store cupboard

1 cup brown sugar

Instructions

1. Preheat an oven to 325^0F then line a baking sheet (extra-large) with a foil and use cooking spray to spray.

2. Spread pecans and cereal on the baking sheet and set aside.

3. Meanwhile, mix sugar and butter in a saucepan and boil for about 2 minutes. Stir frequently.

4. Pour the caramel mixture over pecans and cereal then toss to coat.

5. Bake for about 8 minutes.

6. Remove, stir, and return to oven and bake for another 8 minutes.

7. Remove and allow to cool. Break any clumps (large) with a spatula.

8. Serve.

Nutritional Facts per Serving

Calories: 357.5, total fat: 22.5g, saturated fat: 9.2g, total carbs: 44.1g, net carbs: 42.8g, protein: 3g, sugars: 18.9g, fiber: 1.3g, sodium: 297.7mg, potassium: 142.9mg

Made in the USA
Middletown, DE
20 December 2019